IoT Security

Practical guide book

By David Etter

Table of Contents

Disclaimer

While all attempts have been made to verify the information provided in this book, the author does assume any responsibility for errors, omissions, or contrary interpretations of the subject matter contained within. The information provided in this book is for educational and entertainment purposes only. The reader is responsible for his or her own actions and the author does not accept any responsibilities for any liabilities or damages, real or perceived, resulting from the use of this information.

The trademarks that are used are without any consent, and the publication of the trademark is without permission or backing by the trademark owner. All trademarks and brands within this book are for clarifying purposes only and are the owned by the owners themselves, not affiliated with this document. **

Introduction

IoT systems carry sensitive organization data; hence there is a need for us to ensure that they are secure. Several issues have been reported as far as IoT security is concerned. A single security mechanism in an IoT system is not good as once it is compromised, the organization will undergo huge losses. IoT security is a multi-mechanism approach. In this book, you are guided on the best mechanisms for implementation of IoT security. Enjoy reading!

Chapter 1- A Brief Overview of IoT Security

Security is an essential issue for us to use IoT connected devices safely and reliably. The problem is coming up with the best mechanism to help us implement the security of IoT in the device, network, and at system levels. With protocols and network firewalls, it is possible for us to manage the high-level of traffic which is in the Internet, but the problem comes in creating a mechanism for protecting the deeply embedded endpoint devices which usually have a specified and defined mission with limited resources for accomplishment of this.

With the rising popularity of IoT, it is expected that a mechanism will be implemented which will tackle the issue of security once and for all. However, no specific silver bullet has been found so far for tackling the issue of security of IoT devices.

The good news is that with the IT security measures which have evolved over the past, we can be sure that our IoT system will be secure. However, such protocols should be implemented according to the unique constraints of the connected devices.

Chapter 2- Threats, Challenges, and Constraints in IoT Security

For us to apply the normal IT security measures to IoT devices, it is good for us to first reengineer them so that they can become more suitable according to the specifications of the IoT devices. A good example for this is blacklisting, since it will require us to have too much disk space so that it can work in our IoT.

Disruption and Debial of Service Attacks

It is always good for us to ensure that there is continuous availability of the IoT-based devices so that we can avoid any potential failures in operations and interruptions to the enterprise services.

Even simple tasks, such as the addition of new endpoints to the network, such as new devices will need the organization to consider some of the attacks which can be carried out on such devices.

The business is expected to come up with measures for ensuring that there is physical security so as to thwart any unauthorized access to the devices which are located outside the security perimeter.

Disruptive cyberattacks, such as the denial of service attacks can have dire consequences to the organization. In case thousands of the IoT devices try to access a website for data which is not present, the customers, who might have been happy with the corporation in the past, might become frustrated, and this can lead to loss customers, poor reception in the market, and even loss of revenue.

Complexity of the Attacks

Consider a situation in which you may be using a thermostat for manipulation of temperature readings in a nuclear power plant. In case attackers gain access to the device and then compromise it, then the consequences might be serious. A huge dilemma lies in us understanding where the vulnerabilities fall on the defined complexity meter, and the seriousness of the threat that they pose. For us to mitigate such risks, a project with IoT devices should be designed bearing security in mind, and security controls should be incorporated. Note that it may be possible that the organization will be using hardware devices and software which they may have never used before, meaning that even the types of attacks which may occur may be totally new to the organization. This clearly explains how risky it may be for us to underestimate the risks which IoT devices may pose to an enterprise.

IoT Vulnerability Management

Enterprises usually face challenges when trying to figure out how they should quickly patch the IoT device vulnerabilities, and how the vulnerability patching should be prioritized.

In the majority of these IoT devices, a firmware update is needed so that the vulnerabilities can be patched, and accomplishing this on the fly can be quite challenging. The enterprises usually experience challenges in deciding on how to deal with the default credentials which are provided when the IoT devices are used for the first time. In most cases, devices such as printers and wireless access points will always come with default user IDs and passwords.

Chapter 3- APIs in IoT

In IoT, the providers of devices, platforms, and services have raised concerns over the devices and channels through which the sensitive data flows.

Management of APIs (Application Programming Interfaces) is one of the key ways in which we can gain control over such data. The popularity of APIs has risen as these are used in most organizations as a way of enabling applications to request data from each other. This shows how good APIs are in integrating businesses.

It is believed that APIs will be the key way for enabling interactions between objects which have been connected to the Internet.

The following are some of the APIs which can help you implement a secure IoT app:

OGC SensorThings API- this type of API allows developers to be able to integrate and access functionality of the OGC SensorThings with the other applications. Some of the API methods in this include retrieval of a list of sensors, access to the connected objects, and return of the connected objects. It also provides us with a platform for data exchange which is based on ISO standards and open geospatial.

Netbeast API- this is a platform which helps us to automate the deployment of the Internet of Things. The API makes use of automated dashboard controls for the purpose of synchronizing the functionality of IoT appliances and devices. It supports the OS hosting capabilities for the embedded devices such as the Raspberry Pi. This API is also capable of supporting a number of platforms, such as Windows and Linux. In this API, both the requests and the responses are transmitted in a JSON format.

Space Bunny API- this is a type of API for the Internet of Things and it is mostly used for the purpose of monitoring live streams, and in control of devices which are located remotely. Some of the features of this API include user management, message queues, data stream separation, and protocol bridging. This API greatly supports industrial application development and a smart home. Exchange of information in this API is done in JSON format, and it uses the API keys for the purpose of authentication.

Kaa Admin API- this API is good, as it enables developers to integrate their own applications with the Internet of Things. The good thing with this API is that it connects you to a platform for an unobscured cloud which we can use for IoT development. Users are allowed to establish a connection via a cloud for management of their devices, smart products, prototype, collect, and then analyze data in real-time, scale the IoT solutions, and be in a position to deploy the IoT solutions anywhere.

Bt.tn API- this is a physical button which has been powered by the AA batteries, and it can be programmed so that we can perform a number of tasks. It provides programmers with a REST API for programming a "press" so as to trigger web events, augment work environments, initiate purchases, and more. The action of the API supports POST, GET, and the PUT HTTP methods.

Samsung ARTIK Cloud API- this is an open platform for data exchange, and it has been designed to bring order to chaos, break down silos, and empowers us so that we can bring the IoT promise to a reality. It allows you to collect, store, and take an action on any data from any cloud service or device.

Wia API- this is just a backed which is based on the cloud and is used for the development of applications for use in the Internet of Things. Some of its features include events collection, device management, analytics, and push notifications. This API is based on REST, and it makes use of tokens for the purpose of authentication. Its data is run in the common JSON format.

Weaver API- this API provides the developers with tools by use of the Weaver Internet of Things frameworks and services. With this API, one is in a position to operate multiple devices regardless of the vendor or brand. It provides the developers with effective, user-friendly, cost-effective, and scalable service for the developer who is establishing a connection to apps with IOT devices such as thermostats, smart bulbs, and more others.

Mnubo API- this is a platform for analytics which aims at improving different kinds of hardware by the extraction of value from the sensor data. This task is accomplished by the collection of object data which has been processed within a cloud environment which is based on Mnubo so as to provide strategic insight. The proprietary software suit for Mnubo is SmartObjects, and this is good in providing us with analytics which are descriptive, predictive, and prescriptive.

DeviceHub API- this API will allow developers to integrate solutions which are available from the DeviceHub platform into their own applications, and to be able to develop IoT applications for a variety of devices. The DeviceHub itself is a Platform as a Service (PaaS) company which enables both hardware and mobile developers to connect and manage multiple devices which are located remotely.

Axway 5 Suite

This is an API delivery and governance solution which one needs for the purpose of unlocking any connected devices. Once you enable device-sensor information and actions, you will just move away from the siloed M2M implementations and then create a new digital business by enabling of the device-sensor information and the actions to be easily consumed by the mobile apps, internal systems, and external partners.

In the IoT, we have data everywhere, and this flows from the devices to the cloud, from the cloud to the back-end systems, from the users back to the devices, and all of these have enabled APIs. The Axway 5 suite for API management usually enables us to govern how data flows, and we are in a position to secure the data we see as sensitive, and the performance which we require for supporting connected homes, connected cars, and the Internet things which are have been connected.

Attacks and breaches which can lead to dire consequences can be prevented with this API. This will also help us adhere to legal compliances and avoid the non-compliance penalties.

Chapter 4- Authentication in IOT

For people to realize the IoT, it has been secure. It is always good for us to protect the data in transit and ensure that stored data is only accessed by the authorized individuals. With the introduction of smart devices, hackers have developed mechanisms which can allow them to steal valuable data which makes companies unique.

With the IoT technology, the process of user authentication is even more prevalent. Consider an application which can help you unlock your car by use of your mobile phone. In this case, you have to be assured that you are the only one who is able to unlock the car.

This shows that we have to ensure that the device users are who they say they are, and that they have the necessary credentials so as to access the necessary information.

Security issues in the IoT can be tackled by leveraging the existing 3GPP network authentication mechanism which is a part of cellular networks. In cellular networks, strong authentication and security systems are used, and they use a Universal Integrated Circuit Card (UICC) for storing the security keys on the side of the devices. The GBA technology provides us with a means for implementing the AKA with GBA, and we will be in a position to generate time-limited session keys during the process of SIM card authentication. Once the keys have been generated, we can use them for creation of a protected communication channel based on TLS.

GBA Technology

GBA is a method for key bootstrap which has been standardized by 3GPP. The protocol provides us with a mechanism for the creation of application or service keys via authentication using the 3GPP subscription credentials.

The GBA is composed of two main components in a network: Network Application Function (NAF) and the Bootstrapping Server Function (BSF). The BSF is used for authenticating the subscriber with a 3GPP subscription with the use of the 3GPP AKA protocol. When the SIM card is inside the device, then it can be considered to have been authenticated. The mutual authentication between your network and the SIM card will lead to generation of the bootstrapping session key (Ks), and this will be used for identifying the device. The device will then make use of the Ks as the root key for the generation of session keys which are specific to application,s and these will help in the provision of GPA-enabled services.

The NAF is used for the authentication of web services, and it has to communicate with the BSF so as to obtain NAF-specific shared key material (KsNAF). Once the NAF obtains BSF, the NAF and the device can make use of it for authentication purposes, and a secure communication channel will be established.

Connecting 3GPP and Non-3GPP Devices Securely

For the transport layer communication to be kept secure, it usually relies on authentication and strong cryptographic algorithms. This means the use of certificates for authentication on the server-side and user credentials like passwords and hard tokens for authentication on the client side. Security protocols are used for the purpose of protecting the data.

In the case of autonomous devices, which are usually operated in public areas, there is a need for us to protect the user credentials from both the network-side and physical attacks. This can be achieved by keeping the execution environment and storage environment secure. However, with complex security configurations, operations such as management of the network may become a difficult task for us. If the number of connected IoT devices increases, this might become very complex.

The security of the IoT devices is usually determined by where they are used and the purpose for which they are used. In some environments, authentication and integrity of data is enough for the IoT devices and data to remain secure, but in other cases, addition security measures are needed. In such cases, you should implement strong security measures which are constrained to the device. One of the key elements of a secure IoT is having a secure and strong identity for each of your entities. However, with some IoT devices, support for some security-related tasks is impossible, or some of the IoT devices may need to consume huge number of resources so as to support the security mechanism.

The best solution to such problems is by use of the GBA technology; this technology employs the mechanism of generation of time-limited keys during a GBA bootstrapping procedure. After authentication to the service, the keys can be used for setting up any type of secure communication, such as pre-shared key based TLS session, between the service and the client. The pre-shared keys which are specific to a service have to be derived from the bootstrapped Ks.

The best devices for implementation of the GBA technology are the ones with (e)UICC, which makes use of 2G or 3G, or even LTE, that is, 3GPP devices. Standard GPA also supports devices with the 3GPP credentials, but without 3GPP radio. However, most of the IoT devices are not made with 3GPP access technologies, and they lack 3GPP credentials. These devices will not be aware of the 3GPP networks, and access to the Internet or intranet will be done via one of the following mechanisms:

- Directly- using a wired or WIFI connection to the Internet.

- Indirectly- via a gateway.

Capillary Networks

Capillary networks form a single building block in the IoT. They are made up of either one or more devices, which include actuators, sensors, and other types of constrained devices which have been connected to a public network via a capillary network gateway (CNG).

In a capillary network, connection of devices can be done by use of a variety of wired or wireless technologies such as LAN, wireless LAN, and Bluetooth. In a typical connection, the CGW is used for connecting the mobile network and the capillary network by use of a 3GPP access.

Such features can be achieved via GBA technology, such as a strong authentication and identification, and since there is no need for user interaction, there is a desire for M2M devices which operate autonomously.

Secure Communication and Authentication with GPA in Capillary Networks

In a capillary network, the CGW is used for aggregating the constrained devices, and we use it for authentication of the network. On the side of the enterprise, the constrained devices are viewed as the resources for our authenticated CGW. The interface between MNO and CGW and the enterprise have to be defined in TS 33.220 [6, which is a 3GPP standard. It is expected that the Ua interface can be expanded in the future, and could be expanded into some other protocols such as Constrained Application Protocol (CoAP) [11].

GBA-based data protection and authentication takes the following steps in capillary networks:

If bootstrapping has not been done, the CGW may choose to do the bootstrapping with BSF proactively, or triggered by the NAF response to an unauthorized request from a device which is non-3GPP.

During the phase for bootstrapping, once the network and the CGW have authenticated each other, the GBA client in CGW and BSF will both generate the Ks. The GBS client will never expose the Ks to the CGW or transferred outside BSF. The time for Ks is limited, as you can choose to configure it in such a way that it will expire after some time. Also, the lifetime of KsNAF which we have generated from the bootstrap session key will not exceed the lifetime of a Ks.

For a GBA-secured service to be initiated with a service, any application in need of using GBA in the CGW will have to ask the GBA client for the credentials which are service-specific, which are T-BID and KsNAF. Note that the latter should be a key which has been derived from the Ks.

The application will then use the B-TID and the Ks which has been derived for answering a HTTP 402 authentication challenge and then go ahead to authenticate itself to the service/NAF. The B-TID is then used by NAF for the purpose of retrieving the corresponding KsNAF from BSF.

The BSF will identify the bootstrapping context depending on the B-TID, and then generate the KsNAF from Ks. The NAF will then be in a position to perform an authentication on the response which is received from the application.

In addition to the use of KsNAF for authentication purposes, the CGW and NAF can make use of this for securing the communication, such as establishment of a TLS session which is based on KsNAF.

Once the CGW receives the protected message, the NAF will get the corresponding KsNAF from BSF and then authenticate the message. Also, CGW and NAF will use KsNAF as a shared secret for the TLS, and before the data can be transferred, a TLS-PSK channel will have to be negotiated.

Note that the hop-to-hop security has to be delivered with the CGW which bears the responsibility for GBA and then use it for the security between the NAF and the CGW. Security between CGW and the constrained device will be determined by capillary network access security and the associated credentials.

Delegated GPA

One usually experiences a challenge on how to extend the data protection and authentication between the CGW and NAF all the way to our end device in our capillary network. An extension to the GBA, named Delegated GBA, can be used for the purpose of creation of GBA session keys which are specific to a capillary device by the use of a device ID which is provided in the end device, in derivation of session keys in CGW. The session keys are an extension of the Ks and KsNAFs.

Chapter 5- Best Strategy for Securing IoT

With a proactive and strategic approach to IoT security, you can easily manage the complexity associated with this and reduce your overall risks.

The first step in implementing IoT security should be conducting a risk assessment which should incorporate the IoT into the overall risk profile. The following security practices and principles will help us reduce the risks and maximize benefits of utilization of new types of the connected devices. They will also help you identify the risks which are associated with the IoT and then take the necessary measures to counter these:

1. Assess the risk

    Begin by conducting thorough research which will help you to identify the risks you are posed to. Each implementation of the IoT is always unique. Even in the case of two companies implementing a IoT system for making their buildings to be more energy efficient, the implementations of the systems in the two organizations will be different.

The following are the basic steps of an IoT risk assessment plan:

- Track the IoT solutions- carry out a thorough audit on the devices, networks, communication protocols, and applications. It is always good for you to be aware of the number of IoT devices present in your organization.

- Determine the security vulnerabilities for each of the IoT elements- ratherthan the devices themselves, it is good for you to assess the networks and communication protocols, the databases and applications, and any other network which the IoT network may be interact with.

- Map out the worst-case scenarios- be sure that you are aware of what might happen in case each of the devices fail or it is compromised.

- Determine whether you can isolate the IoT devices and data- in some networks, it is possible for one to operate the traffic and IoT operations separately, but in others, you have to integrate these. An example of this is the HVAC sensors and systems, as these can be operated on networks which have been separated from the core IT applications and networks of the firm. The aim behind this should be to minimize how your database is exposed.

- Determine the sensitivity of data from each IoT device- it is always good for you to be aware of how sensitive data generated, aggregated, or communicated by the various IoT devices is. After that, you will be in a position to tackle the issue of IoT security intelligently.

2. Ensure that both information and connected devices are secured

Most of the traditional IT security measures are geared towards protecting information from corruption, theft, and exposure. Based on the IoT solution, your primary concern may not necessarily be securing the information. An example of this is that data sent by a RFID tag on a package which is in transit may have too little value to an outsider, meaning that you don't have to implement complex security measures for such. Even after aggregation of such data from hundreds of devices, the effect may too minor even after compromising it.

However, if you have the sensor being part of a health monitor worn by a particular patient, the criminals may need to steal such data. In such a case, the data has to be adequately secured by use of security measures such as encryption, firewalls, network tools and other necessary tools.

Rather than merely protecting the data, IoT goes beyond this, and we should have mechanisms for protecting us against any device-related risks. Rather than generating data, the IoT devices will also interact with the devices in the real world, such as when the devices are used for controlling the flow of electricity or water. This explains why you have to consider both operational security concerns and information security concerns.

Once you know the amount the amount of damage which can result after the occurrence of a security breach, you will take the necessary measures to stay safe.

3. Keep the IoT strategy and security in alignment

Recently, organizations began to believe that both business and IoT strategies should be integrated together. As far as IoT initiatives are concerned, this integration is working correctly. A research study carried out by AT&T has shown that most organizations prefer integrating both IoT and business strategies.

Despite how successful businesses have become as a result of such a reunion, it is prone to a number of risks. The organization has to exercise too much effort from the top down when implementing the reunion, otherwise, the effectiveness of the IoT deployment will be greatly undermined. Such a reunion needs attention from not only the IT security team of the organization but also the business units, the chief executive officers, and the board of directors for the organization. With this, the speed, scope, and impact of the reunion will be felt greatly.

4. Determine the Legal and Regulatory Issues

Whenever you are determining the risks and security demands for your organizations, you should also determine the security regulatory requirements that are expected from the organization. An example of this is when the credit card information for the customers of a business is stolen or exposed. In such a case, there are penalties, which might mean closure of the business. If a particular IoT device is manipulated so as to cause physical harm, then its consequences may surpass the ones associated with a breach on the organization's information.

In case you are using different vendors in your implementation for the IoT, then it will be good for you to determine the level of security for each of the vendors. In such cases, it is always good for you to involve the board.

Securing the Connected Devices

For us to ensure that our connected IoT devices are kept secure, we should consider the following factors:

1. Firmware/software update- for each device which has been connected to the network, we should ensure that the necessary vendor is allowed to perform an update to the software of firmware of the device. However, as this update continues, cryptographic checks should be done so as to ensure that we only get updates from the authorized vendors.

2. Reset of the system- each of the IoT devices should allow to be reset back to its original state as manufactured by the vendor.

3. Avoid use of default passwords- hackers and other attackers usually take advantage of default passwords to gain access into IoT devices. The default passwords should be disabled, and users allowed to create unique and secure passwords which should also be kept secure.

4. No use of backdoors- some devices have some hidden or known entry points which attackers can take advantage of so as to harm their IoT system. It is always good for you to ensure that your IoT connected devices do not have such entry points.

5. Avoid use of ancillary services- if a device is not capable of supporting the functions of a service, then these should not be offered on the network.

6. The basic support label- each of the connected devices should have a label guiding the user on how to get support from the manufacturer.

7. Support forum and contact information- a support forum or the contact details should be provided by the vendor which the operator can use to contact them in case something strange occurs.

Chapter 6- Secure Boot

A secure boot forms the root of trust in the IoT and the cornerstone of trustworthiness in electronic devices.

Trusted Software is of Great Importance

One way us to stay safe against attacks which work by breaching the casing of electronic devices is using a microcontroller which will begin to execute from the internal and immutable memory. However, not all device setups have the capability to support this. The software which has been stored in the controller is usually considered to be inherently trusted, since it impossible for any attacker to modify it.

We can achieve such protection by the use of a read-only memory (ROM). Also, the flash memory stored internally in the microcontroller can be used for storage of root-of-trust software, if there is suitable security. Either you can have a flash memory declared non-modifiable once the software has been written to it, or a proper authentication mechanism has been implemented so as to ensure that only the authorized individuals write the software to the flash memory.

If the early software is modifiable with no control, there will be no guarantee of trust. In this case, the "early" means that it is the software which will be executed first once the microcontroller has been powered on. This calls for inherent trustworthiness for this software. If the software has some trustworthiness, then we can use it for verification of the signature of our app before we can relinquish the control of our microcontroller.

Booting into Secure State

After powering on the device, the microcontroller will begin to run the root-of-trust code from a location which is trusted, such as a trusted internal flash or ROM. The primary task of the code is to start the code for the application once the signature has been successfully verified. The signature is verified using a public key which had been loaded in the microcontroller previously by the use of the self-certification of hierarchical certification.

The protected microcontrollers can still be used in the usual manner by software developers for creating software, loading, and then executing the software via the JTAG, and for debugging. If the microcontroller is secure, then the work of development should not be hard.

The identity, authenticity, and integrity of a public key can be ensured in a number of ways. These include the following:

1. Self-certification- the recipient of the digital content will receive the public key in person from the sender, or the sender looks for a mechanism by which to send the public key with no doubt that it is from the right source. The key is then stored in a secure storage so that it cannot be accessed or modified by unauthorized parties.

2. Hierarchical certification- in this method, the public key's origin is verified by a hierarchy of verifiers. Such hierarchies are provided by Public key infrastructures (PKIs). The physical association between identity of key owner and the public key is known as a certificate. The intermediate entities of the public key infrastructure hierarchy usually sign the certificates.

Consider a situation in which an individual needs to have a certified public key. He or she should generate a pair of keys and then keep the private key in a protected place. A certification authority will then meet the individual and then thoroughly verify his or her identity. If the authentication succeeds, the identity information will be attached to the resulting document and then the private key of the authority will be used for signing the document. The identity information will then be bound permanently to the public key.

The signature which results will be attached to the certificate. If somebody tampers with any of the elements, that is, the public key value, the identity information, or the certificate signature, then the certificate will be rendered as invalid. This means that the information in the certificate is not trustworthy. The public key of the certification authority can be certified by another certification authority.

The validity of a certificate will be verified using a similar cryptographic verification scheme such as for dome digital content. The verification of signature is a guarantee on the authenticity and integrity of the certificate and information in the certificate, which is the identity and the public key.

Release of Software and Signing of Code

Once the software has been finished and tested, audited and then signed by an interval validation authority or certification authority, it has to be released. However, for the software to be released for a secure boot, an addition step is needed, which is a binary executable code signature. Once the code has been signed, it will be sealed and authenticated.

We have to seal the code since if it is manipulated, then the associated signature will be rendered invalid since we will not have complete integrity of the digital signature. The authentication of the code is done, since it was signed by an undisclosed, unique, private key which was protected by the owner, which is the person in charge of signing the code. After approval of the software by both internal and external validation authority, then it will be impossible for it to be changed.

Owning the Device

To take ownership of a device, we have to personalize the root of trust in the microcontroller which is the immutable code responsible for handling the secure boot. Also, we have to load the public code verification key which the software approver owns into the device. This key is very fundamental, and it has to be trusted.

The root of trust can be personalized in two ways. In one of the approaches, we will have to use a small key hierarchy, while in the other approach, we don't use any key.

In our first approach, the root of trust for our device already has a root public key verification key. This key has to be hardcoded in the root of the trust, and we have to use this for verification of public code verification key (CVK). As a result of this, the public CVK has to be signed before we can load it into the microcontroller. For the signature operation, the entity to perform the signing should be the root of the root of trust, which should be the owner of the private key which matches the public key which has been hardcoded in the root of the trust.

After loading and acceptance of the public CVK by the root of trust, the key for the root of trust will no longer be used, except for rechecking the CVK internally during each boot for ensuring that it has not been corrupted or modified, or in the case of updating the public CVK. The CVK will then be used for the purpose of verifying the binary executable code.

There is a great benefit associated with the personalization step, that is, execution in an insecure environment is possible since we can only load a correctly signed public key into the device.

A second approach for personalizing the root of trust is achieved by the use of no key. Note that the public CBK has to be loaded into an internal memory which can only be written by trusted software which is executing in the internal memory, or into a non-modifiable memory such as one-time programmable (OTP) memory or the locked flash memory in a secure environment. You must use a trusted environment for ensuring that the intended public key is not replaced by use of a rogue key, since we cannot use the root of trust for verifying the key. A checksum should also be used for the purpose of protecting the key internally so as to ensure that there are no integrity issues with the key. Alternatively, for you to save precious OTP space, we can keep the key in an unprotected place, but the corresponding checksum value should be stored in an internal OTP memory.

A multiparty signing scheme can be adopted in which several entities will be allowed to provide a signature to the executable code. A complex hierarchy can also be implemented in which different code verification keys will be used, as well as intermediate code verification keys and multiple root keys. The ultimate process which is used will be determined by the security policies and the context which the application requires.

During the process of personalization, other options for the microcontroller can be set permanently, such as disabling of the JTAG. Although the JTAG is of great importance during development, we should turn it off for the production parts; otherwise attackers will be in a position to bypass the root of trust.

Downloading App Code

During the manufacturing process, we should load the signed/sealed binary executable code into our device. With a public key, we get advantages since there is no need for diversification, and there is no involvement of any secret.

Since the software approver signs the binary executable code, it is not possible for the code to be modified.

It means that the binary executable code which has been signed can be loaded anywhere. The electronic devices will load and execute this code only, but the other binary executable codes will be rejected. The use of public key cryptography in this process is of great significance, since there will be no need for us to impose any constraints during the manufacturing process.

Deployment of secure-boot devices into the environment is done similarly to the other devices. However, for the executable code to be updated in the field, you have to use the private key of the software approver so as to sign it, and then load it into your device by the use of the necessary means, such as a network link or local interface.

In case the signing key for the software approver is compromised, it will be possible for you to replace the associated public CVK in the field as long as the new key has been signed by the public-key verification key. However, once the root key has been compromised, then it will not be replaceable. However, with good private key management mechanisms, this risk can be mitigated.

Cryptography Alone isn't Enough

Suppose that you adhere to the proper key management and protection practices. Also, assume that there is no guarantee for manufacturing security, confidence, and trust. Also, assume that you have chosen the best encryption mechanisms such as standardized algorithms, high-quality random numbers, and long-enough keys. However, some serious threats can easily expose the assets of the device.

The storage of the public key is done in a location in the flash memory which has been locked, meaning that this cannot be modified anymore. If the preprogrammed public key's integrity or secure boot is been implemented based on the lock mechanism in the OTP memory or flash memory, then the strength of the integrity will be determined by the strength of the lock technology. If an attacker is capable of defeating this technology, then they will be in a position to defeat the integrity of the targeted asset.

Also, it is good for us to carry out a software check on the digital signatures. There exists numerous ways for verification of the software in addition to compliance to the algorithm. Some of these methods are robust, while others are not. Robustness in this case refers to resistance to mistakes, unexpected errors, corrupted bytes, and abnormal environmental conditions. With validation on the hardware and software components of the device, such constraints will be handled properly.

Also, robustness can also be used to refer to resistance deliberate, specific, focused attacks. Such attacks can be carried out maliciously with no real knowledge regarding the platform. The attack can also be carried out after the device has been thoroughly studied. In each of such instances, the attacker is geared towards identification of a weakness associated with the device, and then converts it into an attack path.

Suppose you have your system in which you have to check for the bounds and the length of the entered data before you can go ahead to process it. Static analysis tools can also be used, as they form a very good practice. Such practices are good for helping both auditors and developers to ensure that they use a high quality code. A good developer is also expected to detect and root out any mismatches in code bytes. However, software developers are rushing to deliver code quickly, and this is why they never go through such checks. Also, such checks will also add time to development, testing, validation, as well as the size of the code, and they are also less critical and less functional when compared to the rest of basic functioning.

Also, after the implementation of communication protocols, buffer overflows may result, even the ones which are seen as being too secure, such as the memory-to-memory copies such as copy from an external flash to RAM before using an app or TLS. The buffer overflows are real attacks to the regular software in operation.

Choice of processes is also another example, and this is always referred to as a fault attack. A check on a digital signature is of great importance as it helps us to detect any failure in the integrity or authenticity of the code. Note that such a check can be done on the location of the bytes, and before they can be loaded into the running memory of the application. However, in some operating scenarios, the byte code has to be performed before the check can occur.

This means that such codes are almost ready for execution, even though they do not match the digital signature. The attacker can skip the step involving the check by triggering a power glitch or any other type of a small and non-destructive fault and this will enable the attacker to run the loaded bytes just as the normal bytes.

The most important thing is for you to know that once you use a single security mechanism, the attackers will be motivated to look for mechanisms on how to exploit it and then gain unauthorized access into your systems. A single security implementation is a characteristic of a weak IoT security mechanism.

Implementation of the Best Solution

In today's world, modern controllers have been implemented, and these feature a root of trust which comes with a preloaded and immutable root key. The root of trust having MRK in the secure microcontrollers is internal OTP, ROM, or the internal flash which has been locked at the memory.

Since the memory technology used for storage of the key is immutable, there will be a guarantee on the integrity of the MRK. Finally, a checksum for the key will have to be computed so as to ensure that a glitch to the key does not happen before the use of the key.

For customization of a preloaded key, the customers have to submit the public CVK to the manufacturer for the signature.

With such a key certification process, it will be impossible for anyone to bypass it.

Chapter 7- Public Key Cryptography

In the IoT, the connected electronic devices have to be secured. With the use of the existing public key cryptography schemes, we can conveniently verify the integrity and authenticity of the digital content. Integrity in this case is an indication that our digital content was not modified since the time of its creation. Authenticity means that the digital content was released by the right individual. These two characteristics are provided by the digital signature and it is needed so that our electronic devices trust the digital content.

A message digest is a mechanism which is highly used for ensuring the integrity of digital content, and this is just a secure hash algorithm. The message digest is just a "super cyclic redundancy check (CRC)," but its output is made up of more bytes. For you to have a secure hash algorithm, you just have to forge some digital content which will produce a predefined hash value.

Note that two different and random digital contents will produce different hash values. The probability of having two different digital contents giving a similar hash value is zero. Also, if a change is made on some bytes of the digital content, then its associated hash value will change. Unlike in CRC, it is impossible for us to add some bytes to the digital content which has been modified so as to have the resulting hash value match the original one, which was for the non-modified digital content.

This is why we should have a hash algorithm given the responsibility of guarding the digital content, it will be impossible for anyone to secretly modify the digital content. The computation of the hash is similar to the computation of a CRC since there is no use of cryptographic keys.

The public key digital signature scheme is used for the purpose of ensuring the authenticity of digital content, in which case a pair of keys is used. Two keys are used, a private key which is secretly stored and a public key which anyone can access. The private key is used for signing of the content. The person issuing the digital content will use their own private key so as to identify themselves as the issuer. Anyone can use the public key to verify the signature of the digital content. The two keys have to be tied together. Once the content has been signed with a private key, a digital signature will be produced, and this will be verifiable by use of a public key. This also means that if you are able to verify a signature by use of a public key, then there is no doubt that a private key was used for signing it up. Generation of a digital signature involves two steps. First, the digital content is hashed so as to get a hash content. The former hash value is then signed by use of a private key of the author which is uniquely owned. The resulting value is then attached to your original digital content.

Conclusion

We have come to the end of this book. IoT security is of great importance. The IoT is just a new technology, and not much has been done in terms of implementing IoT security. The devices used in the IoT are vulnerable to attacks. So far, no single mechanism has been established and declared to be the best solution to IoT security. However, research is still undergoing so as to solve the issues. Only the traditional IT security measures are used for implementation of IoT security. For instance, one should ensure that the IoT devices have a well-made authentication mechanism.

This will ensure that only the authorized users have access to the data, and this will ensure that there is data integrity. It is recommended that one should not rely on a single security mechanism for protection of IoT devices. This is because in case an attack occurs, then the effect to the organization will be tremendous. Each organization should also collaborate with the device vendors who may assist in case an attack occurs.